AMERICA'S ARMED FORCES

The U.S. COAST GUARD

DENNIS L. NOBLE

WORLD ALMANAC® LIBRARY

Please visit our web site at: www.worldalmanaclibrary.com
For a free color catalog describing World Almanac® Library's list of high-quality books and multimedia programs, call 1-800-848-2928 (USA) or 1-800-387-3178 (Canada). World Almanac® Library's fax: (414) 332-3567.

Library of Congress Cataloging-in-Publication Data

Noble, Dennis L.
    The U.S. Coast Guard / by Dennis Noble.
      p. cm. — (America's armed forces)
    Includes bibliographical references and index.
    ISBN 0-8368-5681-3 (lib. bdg.)
    ISBN 0-8368-5688-0 (softcover)
    1. United States. Coast Guard—Juvenile literature. 2. United States. Coast Guard—Vocational guidance—Juvenile literature. I. Title: United States Coast Guard. II. Title.
III. Series.
    VG53.N63   2004
    363.28'6'0973—dc22   2004042792

First published in 2005 by
World Almanac® Library
330 West Olive Street, Suite 100
Milwaukee, WI 53212 USA

Developed by Amber Books Ltd.
Editor: James Bennett
Designer: Colin Hawes
Photo research: Sandra Assersohn, Natasha Jones
World Almanac® Library editor: Mark Sachner
World Almanac® Library art direction: Tammy West
World Almanac® Library production: Jessica Morris

Picture Acknowledgements
U.S. Coast Guard: cover, 4, 5, 7, 9, 10 (U.S. Coast Guard Museum), 15, 16, 17, 18, 20, 21, 22, 24tl, 25, 26, 28, 29, 31, 32, 33, 34, 35, 36, 37, 38, 40, 41, 42, 43; U.S. National Archives: 6, 11, 12, 13, 24b, 30; Corbis: 8, 27; Topham Picturepoint: 14, 19 (EANA/The Image Works); NSA: 23.

Printed in Canada

1 2 3 4 5 6 7 8 9 08 07 06 05 04

This book is for Kyle M. Ritten, Kayleigh D. Ritten, and Makayla L. L. Rose

Author Acknowledgements
I would like to thank three people at the U.S. Coast Guard's Historian's office: Dr. Robert M. Browning, Jr., Scott T. Price, and especially Christopher Havern. Three other people gave me great help: Loren A. Noble, Kathleen C. Ritten, and Kyle M. Ritten.

About the Author

DENNIS L. NOBLE spent a total of twenty-one years with the U.S. Coast Guard, serving in a variety of shore stations throughout the United States as well as traveling to the Arctic and Antarctic several times. After retirement he earned a Ph.D. in U.S. history from Purdue University, West Lafayette, Indiana. He now writes full time on the U.S. Coast Guard and related subjects. He lives in Sequim, Washington.

Table of Contents

Introduction

Right: Cadets at the U.S. Coast Guard Academy prepare to perform the time-honored morning routine of raising the flag.

W hat United States naval force operates ships and aircraft to protect the United States, but is older than the U.S. Navy? The answer is the U.S. Coast Guard. Although small compared to the other armed forces, with around 40,000 active-duty men and women, the service has always had many important and unusual missions. It has even fought pirates.

The U.S. Coast Guard is actually made up of several small government organizations that historically dealt with the sea. After the Revolutionary War, the United States disbanded its navy. In an effort to prevent **smuggling**, the U.S. Revenue **Cutter** Service was formed in 1790 and patrolled the East Coast of the new United States. One of the first acts of Congress, in 1789, was to establish lighthouses to help ships safely enter harbors. As a result, the U.S. Lighthouse Service was created. Buoy tenders, ships that set **buoys** for marking safe passages in rivers and harbors, were the responsibility of the U.S. Lighthouse Service.

The sea is a dangerous place. In the United States, early volunteer organizations sprang up to save survivors from shipwrecks. In 1878, the government established the U.S. Life-Saving Service. Its sole mission was to save those in danger of drowning. Early steam-powered ships often posed a great danger. Boilers, used to make the steam for propulsion, were unreliable and apt to explode, causing many injuries on America's waterways. (American writer Mark Twain worked as a river pilot on the Mississippi River. Twain saw many deaths, including his brother's, caused by boiler explosions.) In 1838, the government established the U.S. Steamboat Inspection Service, which inspected ships to make sure they were safe.

These four government organizations, the U.S. Revenue Cutter Service, Lighthouse Service, Life-Saving Service, and Steamboat Inspection Service, eventually merged to become the U.S. Coast Guard. Unlike the Army, Navy, Marine Corps, and Air Force, many of the U.S. Coast Guard's missions include what are considered peacetime duties. Because of this, the service is constantly involved with primary duties that do not include war.

Below: A U.S. Coast Guard fast 25-foot (7.6-meter) boat patrols New York Harbor.

Chapter 1
Law Enforcement and
Early Military Operations (1789–1915)

Right: Alexander Hamilton, the first Secretary of the Treasury. In 1790 Hamilton recommended the formation of the U.S. Revenue Cutter Service to stop smuggling from the sea into the new United States.

The first Secretary of the Treasury, Alexander Hamilton, realized the new United States was losing money to smugglers. Smuggling goods to avoid paying taxes on them began before the Revolutionary War. During the war, many felt smugglers did a patriotic duty by keeping money from England. Once the war was over, however, Congress passed a tax in 1789 on imported goods. This measure, unfortunately, had no impact on the smugglers, who continued their **illicit** activities. To stop this loss of **revenue**, Hamilton sought to establish a **maritime** police force to uphold customs laws. He also sought money to build 10 boats for the police force. The boats would patrol from New England to Georgia and be "armed with swivels." Swivels were small cannons on revolving bases that could fire in any direction. Congress authorized Hamilton's request on August 4, 1790, with the creation of the U.S. Revenue Cutter Service.

The first ten boats, none longer than 60 feet 9 inches (18.5 m), were known as cutters. Designed for fast sailing, cutters could also enter shallow waters. All

Left: The *Massachusetts* was one of the first ten ships, known as cutters, used by the U.S. Revenue Cutter Service.

vessels of the U.S. Revenue Cutter Service, even when steam power removed the need for sails, became known as cutters. Today, the U.S. Coast Guard still calls any of its vessels more than 65 feet (20 m) in length a "cutter." Any craft less than 65 feet (20 m) receives the classification of "boat."

Early Missions of the U.S. Revenue Cutter Service

One of the early missions of the U.S. Revenue Cutter Service was battling pirates. In the early nineteenth century, pirates operated in New Orleans, the Florida Keys, and the Gulf of Mexico. In 1819, the service received two new cutters, the *Alabama* and the *Louisiana*, to combat the pirates.

Slavery was an issue that divided the nation long before the Civil War (1861–1865) erupted. In the North, slavery was unpopular, both because of the humanitarian views held by many Northerners and the fact that industry in the North did not have a use for slaves, unlike the plantations in the South. In 1794, Congress passed the Slave Trade Act, prohibiting the manufacture, fitting, equipping, loading, or dispatching of any vessel to be employed in the slave trade. As a result, the revenue cutters received orders to enforce this Act and prevent any new slaves from being transported by ships, called "slavers," into the United States. Slavers were ships from any country, including the United States, that tried to bring slaves into the country. By the time the Civil War ended, cutters had captured many slavers and freed about 500 slaves.

Below: Slaves being brought ashore at Jamestown, Virginia, from a Dutch slaver.

The Quasi-War

By the time The Quasi-War with France (1798–1801) had begun, the United States had created an official navy. The Quasi-War was essentially an undeclared naval war between the United States and France. With the beginning of the French Revolution in 1793, British warships began interfering with American trade with France, and French warships with American trade with

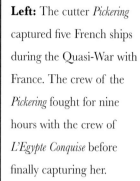

Left: The cutter *Pickering* captured five French ships during the Quasi-War with France. The crew of the *Pickering* fought for nine hours with the crew of *L'Egypte Conquise* before finally capturing her.

Great Britain. Furthermore, the new government of France viewed a 1794 commercial agreement between the United States and Great Britain, known as Jay's Treaty, as a violation of France's 1778 treaties with the United States. The French increased their seizures of American ships trading with their British enemies. As a result, in 1799, Congress gave its approval for the president to order the U.S. Revenue Cutter Service to cooperate with the U.S. Navy whenever it was deemed necessary.

During The Quasi-War, eight cutters fought with the new United States Navy against France. American naval forces captured 20 French vessels, with cutters capturing 16 of the ships. From The Quasi-War until 1915, the U.S. Revenue Cutter Service participated in every naval war of the United States. During the Seminole War of 1836–1839, for example, nine revenue cutters worked with the U.S. Army and Navy. The Seminoles were a group of native peoples who lived in what is now northern Florida. Settlers from Georgia wanted the Seminoles' land. The Seminoles, understandably, refused to give up their land. Eventually, events led to skirmishes between United States troops and the Seminoles. Revenue cutters transported Army troops up rivers and into swampy areas.

Cutter *Eagle's* Battle in the War of 1812

Captain Frederick Lee commanded the cutter *Eagle* at New Haven, Connecticut. On October 11, 1814, the *Eagle* set out to rescue an American ship captured by the British. Forty men volunteered to set sail with the crew. After searching all night, early the next morning Captain Lee and his crew spotted the British ship *Dispatch*, which could easily outsail the *Eagle* and capture it. Captain Lee took an unusual action. He ordered the *Eagle* driven ashore on Long Island, New York. He had his cuttermen and volunteers take the cannon off his cutter and drag the guns up a high bluff. From nine in the morning until two in the afternoon, the cutter's crew fought the *Dispatch* from the shore. At one point during the five-hour battle, the cuttermen and volunteers ran low on wadding for their guns. (Wadding is a soft mass of fibers used for padding.) Members of the crew volunteered to go back aboard the cutter to obtain more. When the new wadding ran out, the crew tore up their log book. When they ran out of shot, the men dug out the British shot that landed in the nearby dunes and fired it back at them. In the morning, the *Dispatch* sailed away and Captain Lee had the *Eagle* refloated. Although it was eventually captured by another British ship, the cuttermen's defense of the *Eagle* became a part of U.S. Coast Guard history.

Right: The crew of the cutter *Eagle* struggled to drag the cutter's cannon ashore. Once the cannon were ashore, the cuttermen fought the British ship *Dispatch* for more than five hours.

Some cuttermen also patrolled on foot through the Everglades, the large swampy area in southern Florida. Eventually, the Seminoles were forced onto reservations in Oklahoma.

War of 1812

The War of 1812 (1812–1815) had its origins in the British practice of impressment, the seizure of American seamen for service in the British navy. The British claimed that they were only seizing British citizens who avoided their military duty by "hiding out" on American ships. The truth, however, was that British and American citizens alike were seized. One source estimates that as many as 6,000 Americans were impressed during this time. President James Madison requested a declaration of war to protect American ships on the high seas and to stop the British from impressing U.S. sailors. The British also seized

Below: The U.S. Revenue Cutter Service cutter *Vigilant* battles the British sloop *Dart* off Long Island, New York, in 1813.

Fighting Pirates

Pirates interfering with trade in the Gulf of Mexico led to the building of the cutters *Louisiana* and *Alabama* to rid the area of the raiders. Both cutters received orders to take station at New Orleans, Louisiana, the home of the notorious pirate Jean Lafitte. On August 31, 1819, the cutters came upon three ships. As *Alabama* approached, the ships tried to outrun the cutter. Captain Jairus Loomis of *Louisiana* fired a shot across the **bow** of the nearest ship, which stopped. A boarding party found that the ship contained prisoners captured by the pirate ship *Bravo*, captained by Jean Lafarge, one of Lafitte's lieutenants. *Louisiana* and *Alabama* set out in pursuit of the pirate. As Captain Loomis' cutter approached, the pirates fired at *Louisiana*. A witness aboard *Alabama* later said, "This continued for a few minutes, when we brought our large guns to bear upon him and gave him a broadside [firing all the guns on one side of the ship], which made all the Pirates run below." Cuttermen boarded the *Bravo* and took possession of the ship.

Right: Pirates prepare to attack and board a merchant ship.

American ships to enforce a trade blockade with their enemy, Napoleonic France. In addition to this, it was widely believed that the British were supplying Native Americans with arms and inciting them to attack American settlers. Neither Britain nor the United States was particularly well prepared to fight this war, however, and the conflict eventually ended in a stalemate.

By the twentieth century, the U.S. Revenue Cutter Service had proven its worth as a seagoing police force. The officers and crews also proved capable naval fighters and eventually received other duties. In 1915, the U.S. Revenue Cutter Service was combined with the U.S. Life-Saving Service. This new service was called the U.S. Coast Guard and remained under the control of the Treasury Department.

Cutters During the Civil War

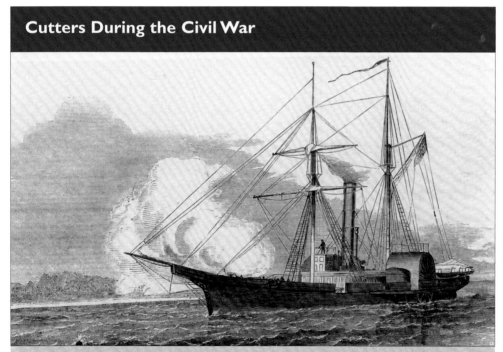

According to an 1864 article in the *Army & Navy Journal*, the U.S. Revenue Cutter Service performed "incalculable service" during the Civil War. Historian Florence Kern points out that the cutter *Harriet Lane*, in April 1861, fired "the first shot of the Civil War from a vessel." Later that same summer, the cutter helped in the first amphibious operations of the war. The operations captured the Confederate forts at Hatteras Inlet, North Carolina. Other cutters served on blockade duty, preventing **materiel** from reaching the South.

Left: The U.S. Revenue Cutter Service cutter *Harriet Lane* fired the first shot of the Civil War from a ship.

Right: Boston Lighthouse, built in 1716, is the oldest lighthouse in the United States.

The United States has always depended on ships bringing in needed goods. Some of the early colonies had built lighthouses to help ships reach port safely. Lighthouses are important to the safety of sailors. For those at sea, lighthouses say, "Here is danger, here is the way to safety, and here is your location." The first lighthouse was built on Little Brewster Island in Boston harbor in 1716. On August 7, 1789, Congress passed a law bringing all lighthouses in this country under the government's control and established the U.S. Lighthouse Service. From a few scattered lighthouses on the East Coast, the U.S. Lighthouse Service grew. By 1910, there were more than 1,397 scattered along the coasts of the United States.

Below: The crew of a lightship relaxes during their off-duty hours. Duty on lightships—"lighthouses that went to sea"—was both isolated and dangerous.

Keeper Kate Walker

The area that Robbins Reef Lighthouse sat on in New York City's harbor was so small that the family of the lighthouse keeper had to live within the lighthouse. In 1883, Kate Walker came to the lighthouse with her husband, John, and son, Jacob. She served as assistant keeper, helping her husband. Three years after coming to Robbins Reef, John Walker was stricken with pneumonia and died. Legend has it that as John was leaving for the hospital, he said, "Mind the light, Kate." Kate did, for the next 36 years.

Kate applied for the position of head keeper. No man wanted the Robbins Reef Lighthouse because of its isolation, but the U.S. Lighthouse Service did not think the four-foot, ten-inch tall Kate could do the job. Her size, however, never hindered her work or in helping others. Kate saved at least 50 lives while at the lighthouse. Kate Walker retired in 1919 and died at the age of 83. A New York City newspaper's report at the time of her death said: "Amid . . . sight of the city of towers and the torch of liberty lived this sturdy little woman, proud of her work and content in it, keeping her lamp alight and her windows clean, so that New York might be safe for ships that pass in the night."

Unfortunately, the management of the lighthouses from Washington, D.C., failed to give the service enough money to properly manage the lights. A lack of money also meant a lack of new equipment. In 1852, a U.S. Lighthouse Board was created. The board established standards of operation and rules for people who worked at lighthouses. As a result, the United States had one of the best lighthouse systems in the world.

Those who worked at lighthouses were known as lighthouse keepers, or just keepers. Eventually, keepers wore uniforms, but all were **civilians**. At many lighthouses, the duty of keeping a bright light was a family occupation. Many women helped their husbands tend the lighthouses. Children also helped their fathers and mothers in running the lights.

In dangerous places off the coast, the U.S. Lighthouse Service stationed lightships to warn of hidden danger. Duty on the "lighthouses that went to sea" was the most dangerous in the service. Lightships often sank in storms or had collisions with other ships due to poor visibility. The U.S. Lighthouse Service also used buoys to mark safe passages in harbors and approaches to harbors. The Service used tenders to supply lighthouses and take care of buoys. Tenders, officially known as buoy tenders, are ships designed to pick up and care for buoys. When steam began to replace wind to power ships, many lives were lost to boiler explosions. In 1838, Congress passed an act that led to the establishment of the U.S. Steamboat Inspection Service. This organization's duty was to inspect boilers and ships for "the better security of the lives of passengers." In 1832, the U.S. Revenue Cutter Service began "winter cruising." Cutters sailed off the East Coast during winter, when storms were at their worst. With the cutters at sea, crews on ships offshore stood a better chance of rescue.

The Guns That Saved Lives

For many years, it was difficult to get a strong rope, called a line by sailors, from the shore to a ship in distress. People tried using kites and shooting a line with a bow and arrow. In 1878, a U.S. Army officer, Major David A. Lyle, designed the device, which bears his name, used by the U.S. Life-Saving Service for many years. This was a small brass cannon, which was loaded with gun powder and shot out a cylinder with a light line. When fired, the Lyle gun sent the cylinder flying to the ship with the line. The range of the gun was about 1,800 feet (550 m). Once the shipwrecked sailors received the light line, they used it to pull out a heavier line. Eventually, a strong rope bridge was stretched between the shore and the ship. The lifesavers then used the breeches buoy or the lifecar to bring the sailors to safety (see page 19). The Lyle gun and its equipment continued in service from the 1870s until the 1960s, saving many lives.

Below: The crew of a U.S. Life-Saving Service station practices with their beach cart. The cart contained equipment for shooting a line from the beach to a ship wrecked near the shore.

Two Unusual U.S. Life-Saving Service Stations

Racial attitudes in the United States until late in the twentieth century prevented African Americans from holding important positions. One U.S. Life-Saving station on the Outer Banks of North Carolina was an exception. When the all-white crew of Pea Island failed to act correctly at a wreck, the Service appointed Richard Etheridge, an African American, keeper of the station. Etheridge's crew consisted entirely of African Americans. From 1880 until the station closed in 1947, African Americans ran the station.

For at least two years, beginning in 1877, the crew of the Neah Bay Station in the Pacific North West consisted of Native Americans. Unlike the Pea Island Station, however, the keeper of Neah Bay was white.

Below: African Americans ran the U.S. Life-Saving Service (later U.S. Coast Guard Station) at Pea Island, North Carolina, from 1880 until it closed in 1947.

A Duty to Save Lives

The U.S. Coast Guard's reputation as lifesavers is due largely to the work first started by the U.S. Life-Saving Service. Saving lives from shore stations started with volunteer organizations. The Massachusetts Humane Society, for example, established the first lifeboat station at Cohasset, Massachusetts, in 1807. A problem soon developed: No one inspected the stations. Equipment was kept in poor condition, and some crews had little experience in boats. Some received their appointment to a station because they knew someone important. Congressman William A. Newell of New Jersey was determined to change this, and in 1848, at his urging, the government established a series of lifeboat stations along the coasts of New Jersey and Long Island, New York. The same problems, however, still persisted. Sumner Increase Kimball, a lawyer from Maine, became the head of the Revenue Marine Bureau in 1871. He made major changes in the lifesaving stations, establishing regulations and providing for paid, professional crews. In 1878, Congress established the U.S. Life-Saving Service and Sumner I. Kimball was put in charge. By 1915, the U.S. Life-Saving Service was a world leader in saving lives from the sea.

Above: Sumner I. Kimball led the U.S. Life-Saving Service from 1878 to 1915. His efforts made the United States one of the leaders in the world in maritime rescue from shore-based stations.

The lifesavers, also known as surfmen, had two means of saving people shipwrecked close to shore. Most often used was the breeches buoy. This looked like a life ring with canvas pants attached. A person would step through the life ring into the pants. Once those on shore saw the person in the breeches buoy, they would pull the device over a rope bridge to safety. The other device, known as either a lifecar or a surfcar, looked like a metal-covered boat. Sailors would enter through a door in the top of the lifecar and bolt down the door. Surfmen then pulled the device safely ashore on the rope bridge. Small rowing boats were also used to rescue people, but this was dangerous work. Usually, the small boats were no longer than 34 feet (10 m), and lifesaving crews often rowed in waves higher than the length of their boat. It was not until 1907 that the Service began to use gasoline engines in lifeboats.

Lighthouse Keepers' Nicknames

For many years, the main source of light for lighthouses was a lamp, which had a wick that extended into oil. A wick is the "string" in candles that is lit to produce flame. A poorly trimmed wick (a wick that is too long or too short) produced a dim light and was a danger to ships. Much of the keeper's time was spent in taking care of the wicks, which earned lighthouse keepers the nickname of "wickies." Even after most lighthouses converted to electricity, lighthouse keepers kept the nickname.

Captain Michael A. Healy

Captain Michael A. Healy of the U.S. Revenue Cutter Service is one of the U.S. Coast Guard's most famous officers. From 1886 to 1895 he commanded the cutter *Bear*, the service's most famous cutter, in the Bering and Arctic Seas, and was one of the first Arctic navigators. Healy kept a secret that he carried to his death. His father was an Irish American plantation owner in Georgia, and his mother was an African American slave. Because of the racial attitudes of the time, Healy's father took his children to Boston, Massachusetts, for their education. This allowed the children to hide their African American heritage. It is possible that Healy would not have gotten the commands that he did and achieved all that he did had it been known at that time that he was part African American. It was not until the 1970s that anyone learned and wrote about Michael A. Healy's racial heritage.

Right: Captain Michael A. Healy, one of the U.S. Coast Guard's most famous officers, commanded the cutter *Bear* from 1886 to 1895 in Alaska and the Arctic. It was learned more than 75 years after his death that his mother was an African American slave.

Surfmen also patrolled the beaches for those in distress, saving many people from drowning. Surfmen maintained beach patrols 24 hours a day during stormy weather, and in the hours of darkness when it was more calm. Surfmen, who despite the fact that they wore uniforms were all civilian employees, would walk patrols of at least 5 miles (8 kilometers) round trip, and sometimes up to 10 miles (16 km). In the event of a wreck, the surfman on beach patrol would light his flare to let the ship know it had been spotted, then rush back to the station to give the alarm.

Above: Pictured in 1908, the crew of the U.S. Life-Saving Service Station at Orleans, Massachusetts, practice in their rescue boat.

Chapter 3
The U.S. Coast Guard (1915–1941)

Right: The crew of an early U.S. Coast Guard cutter pose proudly for the camera.

After the formation of the U.S. Coast Guard in 1915, the combined duties of the former services changed very little. As World War I progressed, however, things began to change. Just before the United States entered the war, two officers saw a future for aircraft in the U.S. Coast Guard. Lieutenants Elmer R. Stone and Norman B. Hall convinced their cutter captain to let them attempt search missions from aircraft. Their experiment was a success. Efforts to obtain aircraft and air stations failed, however, because Congress would not give the money required for the stations and aircraft.

On April 6, 1917, the U.S. Coast Guard came under the control of the U.S. Navy for the duration of the war. During the war, six cutters joined Naval forces in European waters, helping to protect ships from German submarine attacks. After World War I, the U.S. Coast Guard became involved in a different type of war: a war against smuggling. From 1920–1933, **Prohibition** was enforced. Prohibition made it illegal to import, sell, or make alcohol in the United States. Vessels of all types tried to smuggle the illegal substance into the

Below: Elizebeth Friedman helped the U.S. Coast Guard break the codes of smugglers of illegal alcohol.

The Woman Who Broke the Rumrunners' Code

Rumrunners used radios to arrange meeting places to transfer illegal alcohol. They also broadcast warnings to other rumrunners. As smuggling increased, the rumrunners developed codes so the U.S. Coast Guard could not learn the meeting points and other information. For help in breaking the codes, the service turned to the Department of Justice. The department transferred to the service an unusual woman, Mrs. Elizebeth Friedman. Mrs. Friedman and her husband, William, were pioneers in cryptology, the study of codes and code breaking. In three years with the U.S. Coast Guard, Mrs. Friedman and her assistants solved 12,000 coded messages. After Mrs. Friedman left the U.S. Coast Guard, she helped break codes sent by Nazi agents during World War II.

Rescue of the *Mirlo*

During World War I, German submarines attacked ships off the East Coast of the United States. On August 16, 1918, a German U-boat, *U-117*, shot a torpedo into the British tanker *Mirlo* off the Outer Banks of North Carolina. *Mirlo* was carrying gasoline, which exploded. Many sailors aboard *Mirlo* died, but some managed to reach their lifeboats. On shore, a lookout at the U.S. Coast Guard Station Chicamacomico, North Carolina, saw the attack. Warrant Officer John Allen Midgett and his crew launched their rescue boat to help survivors. As Midgett and his crew came upon the location, they found the sea on fire from the gasoline lying on the water. Flames shot high into the air, and dense smoke made the lifesavers choke. Despite great danger, Warrant Officer Midgett and his crew entered the inferno and managed to save the sailors who were still alive. Later, the captain of *Mirlo* said the lifesavers had "done one of the bravest deeds which I have seen."

country. The vessels, as well as the people smuggling the alcohol, became known as "rumrunners." Although the Coast Guard prevented some shipments of illegal liquor, it was not completely successful. The U.S. Coast Guard had too few ships and men to do the job properly. In addition, Prohibition was an unpopular law to try to enforce. Aircraft were also used to help locate smugglers

Right: A U.S. Coast Guard-manned destroyer (left) chases a rumrunner during the Prohibition era.

Ensign Charles L. Duke Captures Rumrunners

Ensign Charles L. Duke and his crew of two men patrolled New York Harbor in a 36-foot (11-m) boat. On July 3, 1927, Duke, with two years of experience in the service, noticed a suspicious freighter with the name *Economy* on its stern. Later, it proved to be the rumrunner *Greypoint*. Duke brought his boat alongside the moving *Economy* and ordered the vessel to stop. When the captain refused, Duke fired two warning shots across the ship's bow with his handgun. Still, the ship failed to stop. Ensign Duke managed to board the freighter. He called out to his crew, "If I'm not out of that pilot house in two minutes, you turn the machine gun on them." Ensign Duke went into the pilothouse of the ship with only his handgun and three bullets. He ordered the captain to stop, but the captain refused. Duke took the wheel himself and ran the ship onto a reef. Ensign Duke then held 22 men for over four hours until additional help arrived. He captured the crew and one million dollars worth of illegal alcohol. Senior U.S. Coast Guard officers said that Ensign Charles L. Duke's single-handed capture was "the most heroic exploit in the effort to stop the rumrunners."

at sea. This use of aviation led to the building of permanent air stations and firmly established aircraft as another tool for the Coast Guard.

In 1933 a Constitutional Amendment ended Prohibition, which caused the number of Coast Guard personnel to be drastically cut. This recognized low point in the history of the Coast Guard lasted until 1939. During that year, President Franklin D. Roosevelt ordered the U.S. Lighthouse Service combined with the U.S. Coast Guard. Meanwhile, technology helped the small-boat rescue stations of the service. All heavy-weather rescue boats now had gasoline engines and radios.

Right: Landing craft laden with troops and Coast Guardsmen in a British port just prior to D-Day, the beginning of the invasion of Nazi-occupied Europe.

World War II (1939–1945) saw the U.S. Coast Guard's greatest international involvement. On September 5, 1939, two years before the United States officially entered the war, President Roosevelt directed the U.S. Coast Guard to carry out neutrality patrols in the Atlantic Ocean. Neutrality patrols were designed to protect American shipping from attacks by German submarines, called U-boats. The Battle of the Atlantic involved Allied warships attempting to locate and sink the U-boats before they could attack merchant ships. The U.S. Coast Guard entered the Battle of the Atlantic with seven new

John Cullen Discovers Nazi Agents

Fog shrouded the coast of Long Island, New York, on the night of June 13, 1942. In the murky darkness, a Nazi U-boat surfaced close to shore, and six agents paddled ashore. Their assignment was to blow up selected targets in the United States. As the Nazis buried equipment in the sand, they heard someone walking toward them.

Seaman Second Class John Cullen, of the U.S. Coast Guard station at Amagansett, Long Island, made his way through the fog on beach patrol. Peering through the fog, Cullen made out the shapes of the men. The leader of the group first said they were fishermen. Then he threatened Cullen, who was unarmed. Next, the leader changed his threat to an offer of money to keep quiet. Cullen took the money and said he would not report them. Once the fog closed in around him, however, Cullen ran back to the station and reported the incident. Soon, the Federal Bureau of Investigation (FBI) entered the case and caught all six men.

Below: John Cullen, left, reported the landing of six Nazi agents on the coast of Long Island during World War II. Here Admiral Russell R. Waesche, Sr., Commandant of the U.S. Coast Guard, congratulates Cullen.

Cutter *Campbell* Sinks a Submarine

On the night of February 21, 1943, a Nazi U-boat sank a merchant ship in a westbound North Atlantic convoy. Early the next morning, a U-boat crippled another merchant ship, but the crew escaped into their lifeboats. Their ship remained badly damaged, but afloat. The cutter *Campbell* left the convoy to help the ship. Soon after *Campbell* arrived, Nazi submarine *U-753* fired another torpedo into the damaged ship. Then, the U-boat fired at *Campbell*. The torpedo missed, exploding just behind the cutter. The crew of *Campbell* retaliated, dropping **depth charges** into the water. *U-753* received so much damage that it could not continue the battle and tried to return to its home port. With the survivors of the ship aboard, *Campbell* started to rejoin the convoy. As the cutter sped to rejoin the convoy, it made sonar contact with another submarine. The *Campbell* dropped depth charges, but did no damage.

That evening, a Polish destroyer, the *Burza*, and a British corvette (small escort ship) attacked the submarine *U-606*. Depth charges from the two ships blew *U-606* to the surface. Cutter *Campbell* located the submarine using radar and attacked. The cutter's guns blazed as the captain, Commander James A. Hirshfield, aimed *Campbell* directly at *U-606*. When the German submarine commander tried to maneuver *U-606* away from *Campbell*, a part of the submarine cut a long gash in the side of the cutter. The crew of the cutter fought until the water entering the *Campbell* shorted out all power. *U-606* sank, and *Campbell*, under escort and with a reduced crew aboard, managed to limp into Newfoundland.

Below: During the Battle of the Atlantic, the cutter *Campbell* sank the Nazi submarine *U-606*.

327-foot (100-m) cutters. According to maritime historian Samuel Eliot Morison, these cutters proved the best escorts during the early phases of the battle.

Conflict in Greenland

In a little-known area of combat, and months before the U.S. officially entered the war, Coast Guard cutters and aircraft battled Nazis in the frigid waters of Greenland. On April 9, 1941, the U.S. Coast Guard became the military service responsible for the defense of Greenland. Greenland, a large, sparsely inhabited island near the North Pole, had major significance during World War II. Greenland has the world's only known sizeable deposit of cryolite, a soft, translucent mineral used in the process of manufacturing aluminum. Furthermore, weather reports from Greenland were important for Nazi operations in Europe. Early on, the Germans had established weather stations in Greenland. In 1941, under intensifying pressure from the British and the Canadians, a meeting of representatives from the State, War, and Navy Departments decided that the United States should participate actively in the defense of Greenland. The U.S. Coast Guard located the weather stations and captured the Germans. In one operation, the U.S. Coast Guard's **icebreaker**, *Eastwind*, in a short battle amid the ice, captured a Nazi **trawler** trying to supply a weather station.

Douglas A. Munro Receives the Medal of Honor

On September 27, 1942, during the battle for the island of Guadalcanal in the Pacific Ocean, 500 U.S. Marines came under heavy attack near a river on the island. The Marines found themselves cut off from their battalion and forced toward the beach. Signalman First Class Douglas A. Munro took charge of more than a dozen landing craft and set out to rescue the Marines. Munro commanded a 36-foot (11-m) landing boat with two machine guns. As the craft approached the beach, Japanese machine-gun fire raked the area. Munro ordered the boats to approach in groups of twos and threes. When the boats neared the beach, Munro ordered machine guns fired at the enemy. Most of the Marines made it off the beach, but a few were still stranded. Munro positioned his boat to cover the stranded men. All the remaining Marines made it off, including 23 wounded. As the last man reached the safety of the landing craft, enemy fire struck and killed Munro. For his actions, Signalman Douglas A. Munro received the Medal of Honor, the nation's highest military medal for valor. He is the only member of the U.S. Coast Guard to receive this high award.

Right: An artist's impression of the fighting on Guadalcanal, September 27, 1942. Pictured in the foreground is Signalman First Class Douglas Munro, U.S. Coast Guard, who posthumously received the United States' highest award for bravery in combat, the Medal of Honor.

Other Wartime Duties

President Roosevelt transferred the Coast Guard to the Navy on November 1, 1941, shortly before the United States entered World War II that December. Men and women of the U.S. Coast Guard served in all areas of the world during the war. Some were aboard transports, others on cutters, and others served at shore stations. Many U.S. Coast Guard personnel landed troops of the U.S. Marine Corps and Army in small landing craft. On the home front, the U.S. Coast Guard patrolled sea and shore for enemy craft and agents. During the landings at Normandy, France, that took place on June 6, 1941, known as D-Day, U.S. Coast Guard patrol boats saved over 1,000 soldiers from drowning. At the end of the war, President Harry S. Truman returned the U.S. Coast Guard to the Treasury Department.

Left: Two U.S. Coast Guardsmen help a battle-weary Marine on board their transport on the Pacific island of Eniwetok during World War II.

Right: A U.S. Coast Guard Strike Team member at the site of ground zero in New York City after the events of September 11, 2001.

After World War II, the U.S. Coast Guard resumed its peacetime duties, but still took part in military actions. Some missions remained the same, but others changed. Soon after the war, the service developed systems whereby lighthouses could run automatically without keepers. In addition, electronic **navigation** systems made some lighthouses unnecessary. By 1985, all lighthouses in the United States operated automatically. Congress, however, required that the oldest lighthouse in the United States, Boston Light, continue with traditional keepers. Many lighthouses were turned over to historical organizations. Today, some people volunteer to work as keepers so that visitors to lighthouses may see a part of history. Buoy tenders and aids to navigation teams also continue to maintain buoys so that ships can reach ports safely.

Postwar Missions

Political unrest in the Caribbean led to unusual duties for the U.S. Coast Guard. Fidel Castro claimed power in Cuba in 1959 after leading a revolution to overthrow the **dictatorship** of Cuba's leader at the time, Fulgencio Batista. Shortly afterward, Castro canceled elections and suspended Cuba's constitution.

Left: The U.S. Coast Guard buoy tender *Hornbeam* approaches a buoy in need of repair near the island of Nantucket, Massachusetts.

Below: A modern U.S. Coast Guard helicopter lowers a rescue swimmer into the water.

Many people living in Cuba worried about the implications of Castro's takeover and fled the country. This led the U.S. Coast Guard to rescue many who set out to sea in unseaworthy craft.

In April 1980, the Cuban government, in a surprise move, allowed

The First Helicopter Mission to Save Lives

On January 3, 1944, the U.S. Navy destroyer *Turner* lay anchored off Sandy Hook, New Jersey. Early in the morning, two explosions resulting from a weapons accident shook *Turner*. The ship sank after the second explosion. Ambulances began bringing in badly injured survivors to the hospital nearest Sandy Hook. The hospital soon faced a desperate need for blood plasma, and snow blocked roads and airfields.

Lieutenant Commander Frank A. Erickson, on duty at the U.S. Coast Guard Air Station, Brooklyn, New York, received a call for help. Senior officers asked if it was possible for the air station's new helicopter to land in a tight location in the Battery (in New York City) and pick up the needed supplies. Lieutenant Walter Bolton, the copilot, helped Erickson fly the small helicopter to the Battery. During the flight, the two pilots flew through low visibility and the helicopter shook from the force of the wind. Despite bad weather, Erickson landed his aircraft. Once the plasma was loaded, however, it added too much weight to the aircraft. The helicopter could not take off. Bolton remained on the ground, and Erickson had to fly the helicopter by himself. Trees and other obstacles blocked his way forward, so Erickson backed the helicopter out over the water. He spun the aircraft around and moved forward. In a few minutes, the blood plasma safely reached the hospital. Helicopters now rescue many victims each year of Cubans to leave the island nation by any means they could devise. What came to be known as the "Mariel Boatlift" led to a flood of people trying to flee by sea. President Jimmy Carter authorized the Commandant of the U.S. Coast Guard to call up nine hundred reservists to help overworked units. Eventually, units of the U.S. Navy also helped. By June 30, 1980, over 115,000 Cubans had arrived in Florida.

The 1990s saw another exodus of Cubans to the U.S., and once again the Coast Guard was called into action. In addition to this influx of Cuban refugees, people fleeing Haiti now required assistance. On November 24, 1995, the cutter *Dauntless* rescued 578 migrants from an overloaded 75-foot (23-m) freighter. This is the largest number of migrants rescued from a single vessel in U.S. Coast Guard history. The work has not slackened. In 2000, the service saved the lives of 3,400 migrants.

Below: One of the U.S. Coast Guard's largest missions is the interception of boats and ships trying to smuggle illegal drugs into the United States. Here a U.S. Coast Guardsman examines the results of a successful "drug bust."

Right: During the Vietnam War, crew members of U.S. Coast Guard 82-foot (25-m) patrol boats boarded and checked vessels off the coast of South Vietnam for smuggled weapons.

The 1970s saw an increase in a mission begun before World War II. Smugglers were bringing large amounts of illegal drugs into the United States by boats. Soon, the service became fully involved in the "war on drugs." This is now one of the U.S. Coast Guard's largest missions. Cutters and aircraft continually work to intercept smugglers.

As in the past, the U.S. Coast Guard continues to serve in the military actions of the United States. During the Korean War (1950–1953), the U.S. Coast Guard served in a support capacity. They provided weather information and communications to ships and aircraft en route to Korea. In addition, U.S. Coast Guard personnel made sure that explosives were safely loaded aboard ships.

During the Vietnam War (1961–1975), the U.S. Coast Guard served in many capacities. Crews aboard 82-foot (25-m) patrol boats helped intercept guns and supplies smuggled from North Vietnam into South Vietnam. To accomplish this, crews aboard the small patrol boats boarded and searched vessels. For ten months beginning in July 1965, for example, crews in the Gulf of Thailand area

The Rescue of the *Pendleton*

On February 18, 1952, a furious storm swept the seas around Cape Cod, Massachusetts, causing two tanker ships to break apart. Cutters and motor lifeboats rescued 70 of the 84 sailors aboard the sinking ships. Thirty-two of the rescued sailors came from the tanker *Pendleton*. Twenty-four-year-old Boatswain's Mate First Class Bernard C. Webber and his crew of three started toward the sinking *Pendleton* from their station at Chatham, Massachusetts. In waves 60 feet (18 m) high, Webber and his men reached the after part of the tanker, where they found 33 sailors. The sailors put a rope ladder over the side, and one at a time climbed down the ladder. The sailors wanted Webber and his crew to bring their small motor lifeboat near the ladder. Then, the sailors would try to leap to the motor lifeboat.

A sailor jumped toward the front of the motor lifeboat, where a crewman caught him. Another sailor jumped, then another. Some sailors missed the small boat. Webber repositioned his boat, and his crew pulled the sailors out of the churning sea. Webber again drove toward the rope ladder to pick up the last sailor. The man leaped from the ladder and missed the lifeboat. Webber saw the man holding on to the sinking ship's propeller. As he moved his boat to pick up the sailor, the sea pitched the motor lifeboat against the man, crushing him to death. With 36 people aboard his small boat, Webber started for shore and safety. Somehow, he managed to bring the sailors safely ashore. For his efforts, Bernard C. Webber and his crew earned the Gold Life-Saving Medal.

Below: The tanker Pendleton broke in half during a furious storm off Cape Cod, Massachusetts, in 1952. The rope ladder hangs from the wreck in this photograph taken after the storm.

Right: A 52-foot (16-m) lifeboat from the Coast Guard Station at Cape Disappointment, Washington, heads out to sea over the Columbia River Bar, a dangerous area of high waves.

boarded over 40,000 craft. Often during patrols the cutters came under fire. On June 20, 1966, the patrol boat *Point League* located a suspicious ship. When the ship refused to stop, a battle between the ship and the cutter began. Another patrol boat, *Point Slocum,* arrived to help. Soon, other U.S. Army and Air Force units arrived. The battle continued for close to eleven hours. Eventually the ship caught fire and grounded on the shore. It contained one hundred tons of ammunition and 1,200 weapons.

During the war, larger cutters stood farther offshore and supported troops with gun fire missions. Some U.S. Coast Guardsmen provided security at the busy ports of South Vietnam, especially around the capital of South Vietnam, Saigon. Part of these duties included the supervision of the unloading of high explosives. Other U.S. Coast Guard personnel provided navigation for shipping in South Vietnamese waters.

The U.S. Coast Guard has served in other military operations since the ending of the Vietnam War, including the invasion of Grenada in 1983, Operations Desert Shield and Desert Storm, and in the former Yugoslavia. Members of the U.S. Coast Guard also served during recent operations in Iraq.

Serving the Environment

A little-known traditional mission of the U.S. Coast Guard began receiving more attention in the 1970s. The service has always helped protect the environment. As early as 1867, it helped protect the Alaskan fur seals from extinction. The service's Bering Sea Patrol helped limit the illegal killing of these mammals. In 1972, the Federal Water Pollution Act led the Service to establish a National Strike Force to fight oil spills. Three strike teams stand ready to go anywhere in the world to help contain oil spills. When deployed, they bring the latest equipment to battle dangers to the environment.

Since their establishment, the strike teams have responded worldwide to potential and actual oil spill sites. Even during war, the U.S. Coast Guard has protected the environment. On February 13, 1991, during the Persian Gulf War, service aircraft mapped over 40,000 square miles (103,500 sq km) of oil spills. Strike team members also helped at the World Trade Center towers in New York City on September 11, 2001, providing the needed knowledge on potential environmental hazards.

The U.S. Coast Guard also helps protect fisheries. One law enforced by the service concerns the use of very large drifting nets, some as large as 25 miles (40 km) in length. This technique is a very destructive method of fishing, as it captures and kills any other unwanted marine life in its way. The method was banned on the world's seas in 1991. In June 1998 three U.S. Coast Guard cutters, U.S. Coast Guard aircraft and two Russian fisheries patrol vessels seized four Chinese fishing vessels which had been carrying out drift-net fishing.

U.S. Coast Guard Aviation

Despite some claims within the service after World War II that seaplanes were the best aircraft for rescue, the U.S. Coast Guard now largely uses helicopters for search and rescue. Some cutters now carry helicopters on patrols. Service helicopters have made amazing rescues. In October 1980, almost 200 miles (320 km) off Sitka, Alaska, the cruise ship *Prinsendam* rocked with explosions. It stopped in the water after fire swept the engine room. The ship's crew put the passengers into lifeboats and lowered them into rough seas. Four U.S. Coast Guard, one U.S. Air Force and two Canadian helicopters hoisted more than five

Right: Two U.S. Coast Guardsmen on board the cutter *Alert* confer before boarding a fishing vessel to enforce fishing regulations.

hundred survivors from lifeboats in the Gulf of Alaska. The aircraft brought the shipwrecked survivors to the cutter *Boutwell* and the commercial tanker *Williamsburgh*. The cruise ship sank seven days later, but not one life was lost.

Today's Coast Guard

In March 2003, in response to the attacks of September 11, 2001, the U.S. Coast Guard was moved to the new Department of Homeland Security. Although its active-duty force is small in comparison to the other armed services, the Coast Guard continues to serve throughout the world and perform its traditional missions.

Men and women join the U.S. Coast Guard for many reasons. Some join to save lives, others wish to work in law enforcement. Yet others enter the service to serve on cutters or to work in aviation. All the men and women follow grooming standards that stress a neat appearance. For example, men must have short, neatly trimmed hair. They may wear short moustaches, but no beards. Woman's hair can touch, but not extend below, the lower edge of the collar.

Women have been involved in the Coast Guard before it was known as the Coast Guard, as lighthouse keepers such as Kate Walker demonstrated. It was not until World War I, however, that a legitimate role for women in uniform was created. On March 19, 1917, the Navy authorized the enlistment of women in the Naval Reserve, a policy that was extended to the Coast Guard since it was under the control of the Navy at this time. According to records, only a handful of women joined the Coast Guard at that time. Today, however, more than a third of the cadets who train at the Coast Guard Academy each year are women. Furthermore, the U.S. Coast Guard is the only American armed force in which women can serve in any capacity.

The U.S. Coast Guard does not discriminate on the grounds of race, religion, or ethnicity. Its policies are

Below: Lieutenant Sandra Stoce, the first female commanding officer of a 140-foot (43-m) icebreaking tug, stands near her command, the cutter *Katmi Bay*, which operates in the Great Lakes.

Sinbad, the Coast Guard's Most Famous Mascot

ARMY MIRACLES
— for You!

How wartime marvels
will make life easier
after peace has come

by Major General
Edmund B. Gregory
Quartermaster General, U.S. Army

Page 4 →

Many U.S. Coast Guard cutters and stations have mascots. There have been dogs, cats, and even goats as mascots. There is one mascot, however, that became a legend. In 1937, the crew of the cutter *Campbell* smuggled a black and tan mixed-breed dog aboard the ship. The dog quickly won the admiration of everyone. Crew members named him "Sinbad." Sinbad became a world traveler and a combat veteran. He served in both the Atlantic and Pacific Oceans. One wartime captain of the cutter said that if "Sinbad left the vessel, half the crew would go with him."

Sinbad served as mascot aboard *Campbell* for 11 years. On September 28, 1948, he left the cutter for retirement at a shore station. At a lifeboat station in New Jersey, Sinbad continued to help U.S. Coast Guardsmen. He died at the lifeboat station on December 20, 1951. The crew buried him by the station's flagpole. Until 1982, when *Campbell* stopped serving in the U.S. Coast Guard, the cutter always had a mascot named Sinbad.

Above: Sinbad, the mascot of the U.S. Coast Guard cutter *Campbell*, was a world traveler and combat veteran. He served on board the cutter for 11 years.

aimed at having the service represent a "slice of America." The service believes a person's sexual orientation is a personal and private matter and will not stop anyone from entering the service or pursuing a career. If, however, a person states he or she is homosexual or engages in homosexual practices, he or she can be dismissed.

The Coast Guard Academy

The U.S. Coast Guard Academy at New London, Connecticut, provides a four-year education to selected men and women. Unlike other service academies, there is no congressional appointment required and tuition is free. Admission to the academy is by national competition. An average of 265 students enter the Academy each year out of approximately 5,500 applicants. The four-year academic program leads to a Bachelor of Science degree in a variety of majors, such as naval architecture and marine engineering, civil engineering, mechanical engineering, or electrical engineering. Those who graduate receive an officer's commission in the service.

Upon graduation, there is a five-year commitment to serve as a commissioned Coast Guard officer. Qualified college graduates and U.S. Coast Guard enlisted people may attend Officer's Candidate School (OCS), at New London, Connecticut, and receive commissions as officers in the service. The highest rank an officer may reach is admiral.

Men and women who enter the service in the enlisted force receive basic training, known as "boot camp," at Cape May, New Jersey. Coast Guard boot camp is run just like any other military boot camp. It lasts for seven weeks and recruits go through various regimens of physical fitness training and classroom work. After finishing their training, qualified enlisted members receive further specialized training at a variety of service schools. The schools teach the skills needed to work in many fields within the service. Enlisted members, for example, may become Marine Science Technicians and work in oceanography and take weather observations. Other enlisted members may learn the skills to become a Machinery Technician and learn to operate and repair a variety of machinery.

Yet others may train to become Photojournalists, learning the skills needed to photograph and describe U.S. Coast Guard activities. The standard term of enlistment in the Coast Guard is four years.

Promotion for enlisted members leads to petty officer grade. The highest petty officer grade is master chief petty officer. Some petty officers receive promotion to chief warrant officer.

Below: Cadets throw their hats in the air at their graduation from the U.S. Coast Guard Academy in 2002.

Time Line

1716:	September 14, Boston Lighthouse, the first in the United States, starts operations.
1789:	August 7, the U.S. Lighthouse Service is established.
1790:	August 4, the U.S. Revenue Cutter Service is established.
1798–1801:	Cutters battle the French during The Quasi-War.
1836–1842:	Cutters help transport U.S. Army troops and assist U.S. Navy during the Seminole Wars.
1838:	August 4, the U.S. Steamboat Inspection Service is established.
1878:	June 18, the U.S. Life-Saving Service is established.
1903:	The Department of Commerce and Labor is established; the Bureau of Navigation and the Steamboat Inspection Service are transferred to the new department.
1915:	January 28, the U.S. Revenue Cutter Service and the U.S. Life-Saving Service are merged to form the U.S. Coast Guard.
1917:	April 6, the U.S. Coast Guard is transferred to the control of the Navy during World War I; six cutters are sent to European waters.
1919:	August 28, President Woodrow Wilson returns the U.S. Coast Guard to the Treasury Department.
1939:	July 1, the Lighthouse Service becomes part of the U.S. Coast Guard.
1941:	November 1, President Franklin D. Roosevelt transfers the U.S. Coast Guard to Navy control during World War II.
1950–1953:	Cutters and U.S. Coast Guard personnel perform a variety of duties during the Korean War.
1967–1971:	Cutters and U.S. Coast Guard personnel perform a variety of duties during the Vietnam War.
2001:	U.S. Coast Guard personnel participate in security-related missions after the September 11 attacks.
2002:	The Coast Guard becomes part of the Department of Homeland Security.
2003–2004:	U.S. Coast Guard personnel participate in operations in Iraq.

Glossary

bow: the front part of a boat or ship

buoy: a floating object moored to the bottom to mark a channel or something lying under the water

civilian: someone who is not on active duty in a military, police, or fire-fighting force

cutter: any U.S. Coast Guard vessel over 65 feet (20 m) in length

depth charge: an underwater bomb, usually used against submarines, which is set to explode at a given depth

dictatorship: a form of government in which absolute power is concentrated in one person

icebreaker: a ship with a strengthened hull, capable of operating in frozen sea conditions

illicit: not permitted; unlawful

maritime: of or relating to navigation or commerce on the sea

materiel: equipment, apparatus, and supplies used by an organization or institution

navigation: the science of getting ships from place to place; especially the method of determining position, course, and distance traveled

Prohibition: the forbidding of the manufacture and sale of alcoholic drink established in the U.S. from 1920–1933

revenue: the yield of sources of income (as taxes) that a political unit (as a nation or state) collects and receives into the treasury for public use

smuggling: to bring something into or out of a country secretly contrary to the law and especially without paying duties imposed by law

trawler: a boat used for fishing with large, wide-mouthed nets

Further Information

Books:

Cooper, Jason. *U.S. Coast Guard*. Vero Beach, FL:
The Rourke Book Company, 2003.

Demarest, Chris L. *Mayday! Mayday!: A Coast Guard Rescue*. New York:
Margaret K. McElderry Books, 2004.

Graham Gaines, Anne. *The Coast Guard in Action*. Berkeley Heights, NJ:
Enslow Publishers, Inc., 2001.

Green, Michael. *The United States Coast Guard (Serving Your Country)*. Mankato, MN:
Capstone Press, 2000.

Weintraub, Aileen. *Life Inside the Coast Guard Academy*. New York:
Children's Press, 2002.

Web sites:

United States Coast Guard
www.uscg.mil/
Learn all about the Coast Guard in action at this site, from the history of the Coast Guard to jobs, to the equipment used.

U.S. Coast Guard Academy
www.cga.edu/
This site contains information regarding the admissions process, daily life of cadets, training, and more.

The United States Coast Guard Auxiliary
www.cgaux.org/
The United States Coast Guard Auxiliary was established by Congress in 1939 to assist the Coast Guard in promoting boating safety.

U.S. Coast Guard: The Shield of Freedom
www.gocoastguard.com/
If you're interested in joining the Coast Guard, this site is an excellent place to find information on scholarships and for finding a recruiter in your area.

Index

Page numbers in **bold** indicate photographs or illustrations